French - Hebrew

LEARNING FLASHCARDS

FOR BABIES TODDLERS

alligator

תַּנִּין

The alligator is having a party.

fourmi

נְמָלָה

The ant is red.

ours

דוב

The bear loves you.

abeille

דבורה

The bee is saying hello.

oiseau

צִיפּוֹר

The bird is flying.

papillon

פַּרְפַּר

The butterfly is pretty.

chameau

גָּמָל

The camel has a hump.

chat

חתול

The cat is happy.

dinosaure

דינוזאור

The dinosaur is laying eggs.

poulet

עוֹף

The chicken is dancing.

vache

פָּרָה

The cow has a bell.

cerf

צְבִי

The reindeer has a toy.

chien

כֶּלֶב

The dog has two floppy ears.

dauphin

דולפִין

The dolphin is swimming.

canard

ברווז

The duck has a bow.

aigle

נשר

The eagle is looking for food.

l'éléphant

פיל

The elephant is sitting.

poisson

דג

The fish is a clownfish.

libellule

שַׂפִּירִית

The dragonfly is blue.

renard

שׁוּעָל

The fox has a red nose.

grenouille

צְפַרְדֵּעַ

The frog is smiling.

girafe

גִ'ירָפָה

The giraffe has a long neck.

chèvre

עֵז

The goat has a beard

ver de terre

תּוֹלַעַת

The worm is in the apple

poule

תַרְנְגֹלֶת

The hen has chicks.

hippopotame

סוּס הַיְאוֹר

The hippo is big.

cheval

סוּס

The horse is fast.

kangourou

קנגרו

The kangaroo has a baby.

chaton

גור חתולים

The kitten is playing.

lion

אַרְיֵה

The lion has a mane.

homard

לובסטר

The lobster is red.

singe

קוֹף

The monkey has a tail.

poulpe

תמנון

The octopus has food.

hibou

יַנשוּף

The owls have big eyes.

panda

פנדה

The panda wears a diaper.

porc

חֲזִיר

The pig is fat and pink.

chiot

כלבלב

The dog is brown.

lapin

ארנב

The rabbit has a carrot.

rat

עכברוש

The mouse is writing something.

crabe

סרטן

The crab has two pinchers.

requin

כריש

The shark is scary.

mouton

כבשים

The sheep are very fluffy.

escargot

שַׁבְּלוּל

The snail is slow.

serpent

נָחָשׁ

The snake has poison.

araignée

עַכָּבִישׁ

The spider is purple.

écureuil

סְנָאִי

The squirrel has a nut.

tigre

נָמֵר

The tiger has a red bow.

tortue

צָב

The turtle has a shell.

loup

זְאֵב

The wolf is smiling.

zèbre

זֶבְּרָה

The zebra is black and white.

dinde

טורקיה

The turkey has two legs.

coq

תַּרְנְגוֹל

The rooster will crow.

perroquet

תוּכִּי

The parrot is colorful.

hérisson

קִפּוֹד

The hedgehog has apples.

pomme

תפוח עץ

The apple has a leaf.

abricot

מִשְמֵש

The apricot is yellow.

avocat

אבוקדו

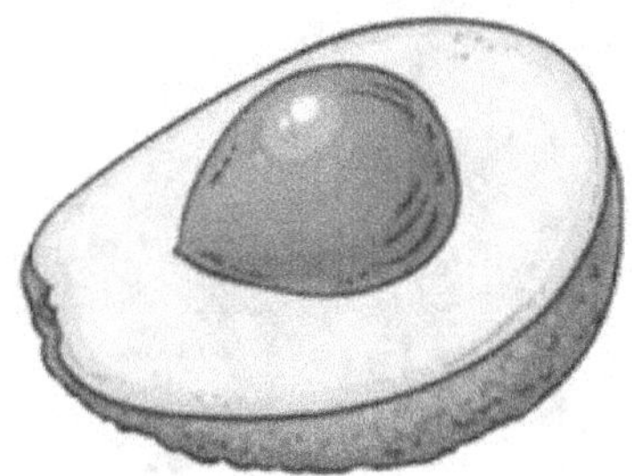

The avocado has a nut.

banane

בננה

The banana is yellow.

la mûre

אוכמניות

There are a lot of blackberries.

cassis

עִנְבֵי שׁוּעָל

The blackcurrants are yummy.

myrtille

אוכמנית

The blueberries are sweet.

cerise

דובדבן

The cherries have a stem.

noix de coco

קוקוס

The coconuts have juice.

figues

תאנים

The fig has seeds.

grain de raisin

עֵנָב

The grapes are purple.

pamplemousse

אשכוליות

The grapefruits are sour.

kiwi

קיווי

The kiwi is fresh.

citron

לימון

The lemons are yellow.

citron vert

ליים

We have lots of lime.

litchi

ליצ'י

I like to eat lychee.

mandarine

תפוז מנדרינה

Oranges are refreshing.

mangue

מנגו

Mango is my favorite fruit.

orange

תפוז

Mandarins are like oranges.

papaye

 פפאיה

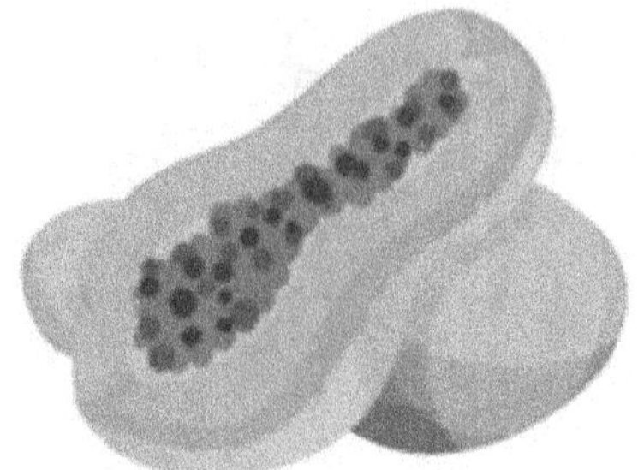

Papayas have lots of seeds.

pêche

אפרסק

Peaches are juicy.

poire

אגס

Pears have a strange figure.

ananas

אננס

The pineapple has a thumbs up.

prune

שזיף

Plums are healthy for you.

grenade

רימון

Pomegranates are all red.

framboise

פֶּטֶל

The raspberry is shiny.

fraise

תּוּת

The strawberry has leaves on top.

pastèque

אבטיח

The watermelon is big.

mandarine

מַנדָרִינָה

The tangerine looks like an orange.

tarte

פַּאי

I like to eat apple pie.

gâteau

עוגה

That cake is huge.

bonbons

ממתק

Candy is not good for your teeth.

biscuit

עוגייה

Cookies are easy to make.

donut

סופגנייה

I like strawberry donuts.

crème glacée

גלידה

The ice cream is melting.

muffin

מַאפִין

The muffin has a cute wrapper.

pudding

פּודינג

We eat pudding on Christmas.

classeur

כּוֹרֵךְ

I keep pictures in my binder.

livre

סֵפֶר

I like to eat books.

sac à dos

תיק גב

The backpack has lots of stuff.

les ciseaux

מספריים

I have scissors in my bag.

épingles

סיכות

Pins can hold stuff up.

agrafe

לְקַצֵץ

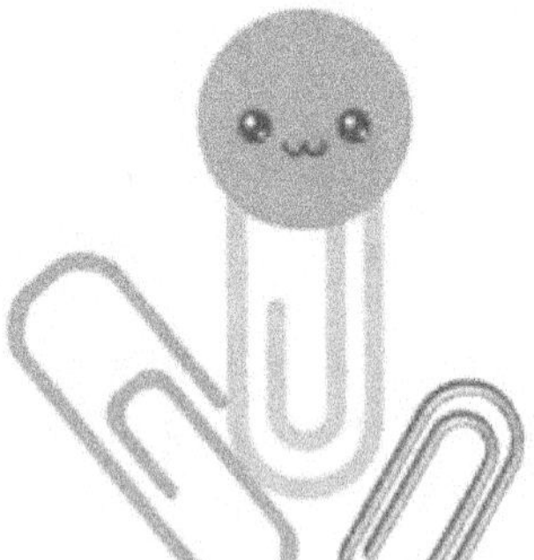

Clips can hold up paper.

papier

עיתון

I have lots of paper.

agrafeuse

מהדק

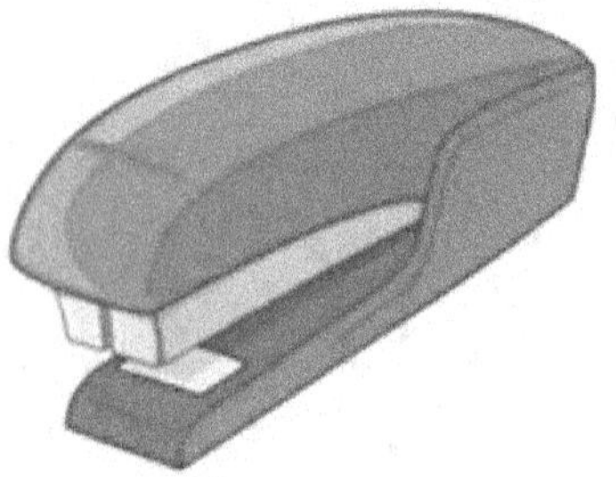

My stapler is shiny and red.

calculatrice

מַחשְׁבוֹן

My calculator has buttons.

règle

סרגל

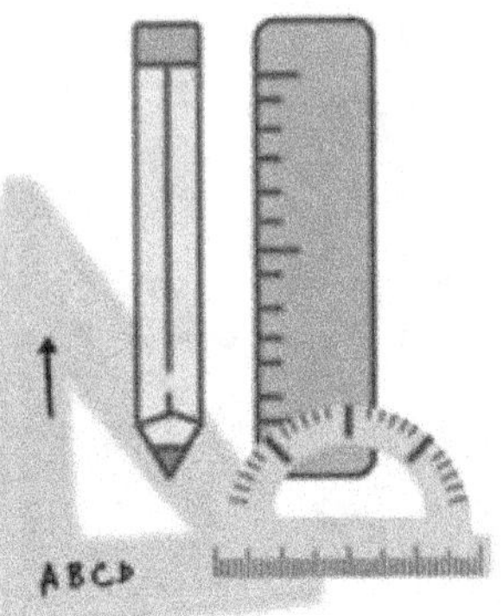

I have lots of rulers.

la colle

דֶבֶק

The glue is sticky.

bibliothèque

כּוֹנָנִית

My bookcase has lots of things.

calendrier

לוּחַ שָׁנָה

I have a calendar on my table.

chaise

כִּסֵּא

My chair is fancy.

l'horloge

שָׁעוֹן

The clock says that it's 3 o'clock.

ordinateur

מַחְשֵׁב

I do things on my computer.

bureaux

שולחנות עבודה

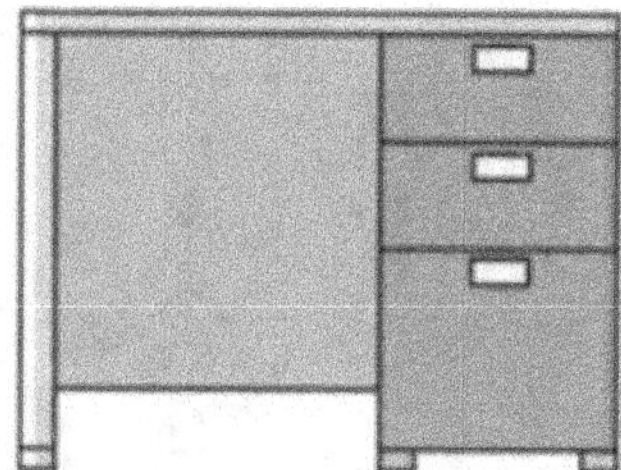

I put lots of things on my desk.

dictionnaire

מילון

The dictionary has lots of words.

la gomme

מַחַק

Erasers are used with pencils.

carte

מַפָּה

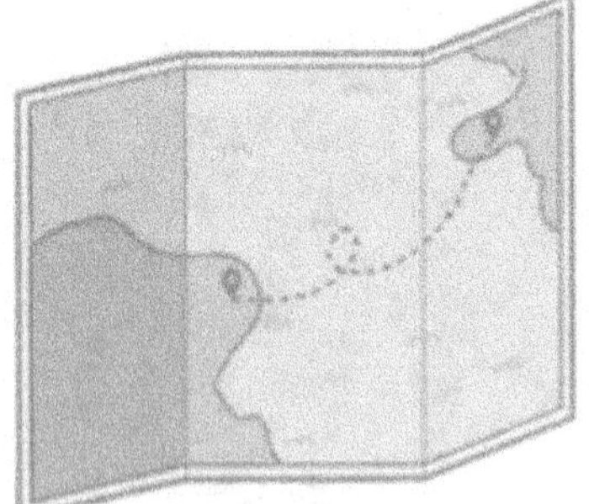

The map shows you different places.

carnet

מחברת

I use notebooks at school.

stylo

עֵט

My pen is very pretty.

crayon

עִפָּרוֹן

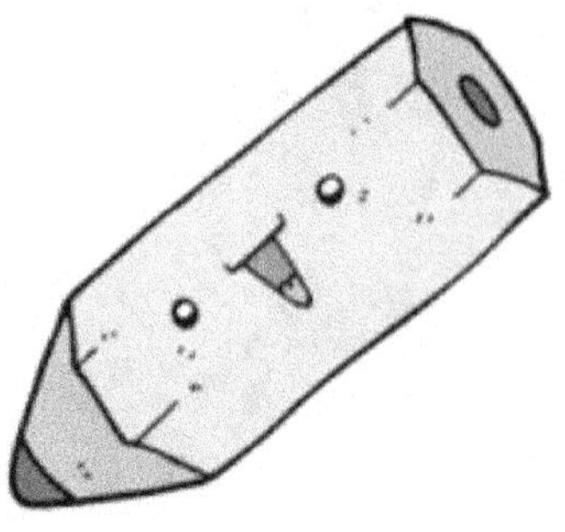

My friend gave me a pencil.

ceinture

חֲגוֹרָה

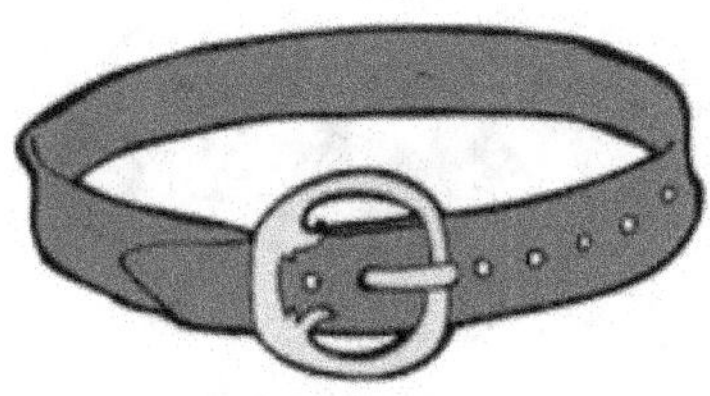

I have a belt on my pants.

bottes

מגפיים

I have big brown boots.

chapeau

כּוֹבַע

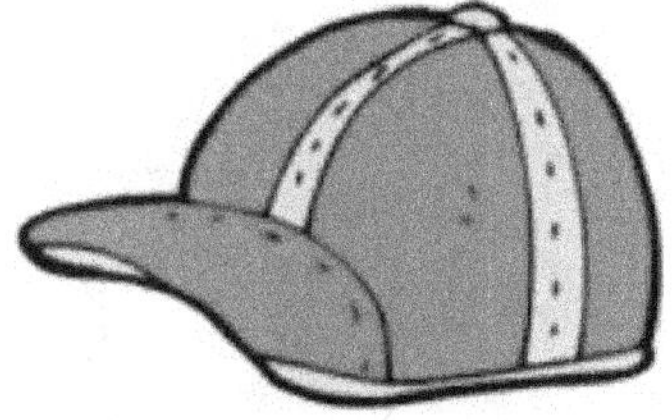

My mom bought me a new cap.

manteau

מעיל

She has a long yellow coat.

robes

שמלות

My dress has a bow.

gants

כפפות

I got new gloves.

chapeau

כּוֹבַע

That hat is for a wicked witch.

veste

זָ'קֵט

The jacket is cozy.

jeans

גִ'ינְס

My jeans are long.

pyjamas

פִּיגָ'מָה

I sleep in my pajamas.

un pantalon

מִכְנָסַיִים

The bear is wearing pants.

imperméable

מְעִיל גֶשֶׁם

We wear our raincoats when it is
raining.

écharpe

צָעִיף

The baby has a scarf around his neck.

chemise

חוּלצָה

I like this shirt the best.

des chaussures

נעליים

I have red and blue shoes.

jupe

חצאית

My skirt has lots of buttons.

pantalon

מִכְנָסַיִּם

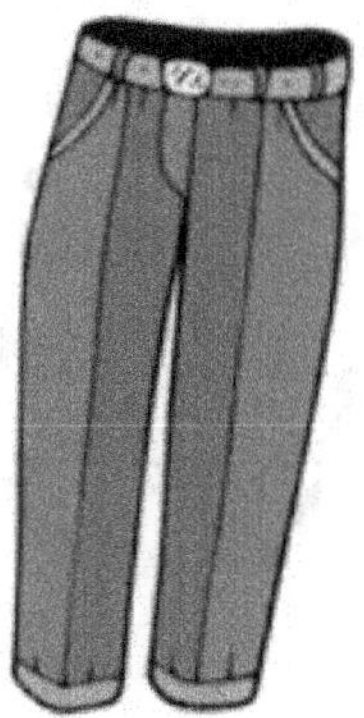

My dad wears slacks.

chaussons

נעלי בית

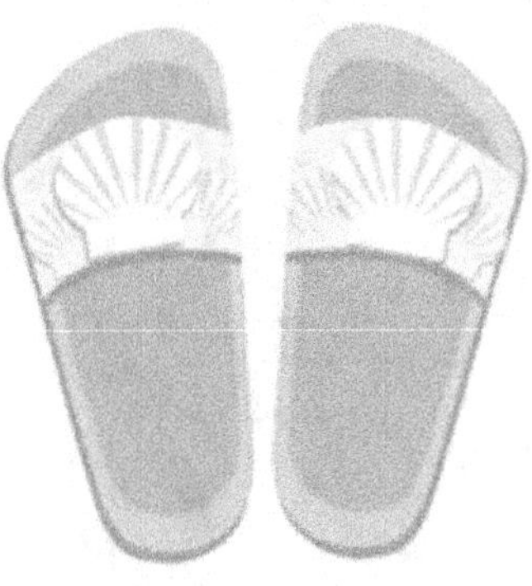

I have seashells on my sandals.

chaussettes

גרביים

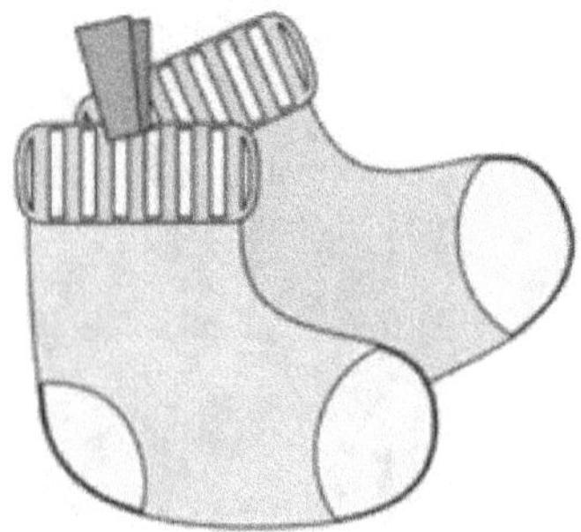

My baby sister wears socks.

costume

חליפה

My brother is wearing a suit.

chandail

סְווֶדֶר

I am wearing a sweater for winter.

cravate

עֲנִיבָה

My dad wears a tie to meetings.

pantalon

מכנסיים

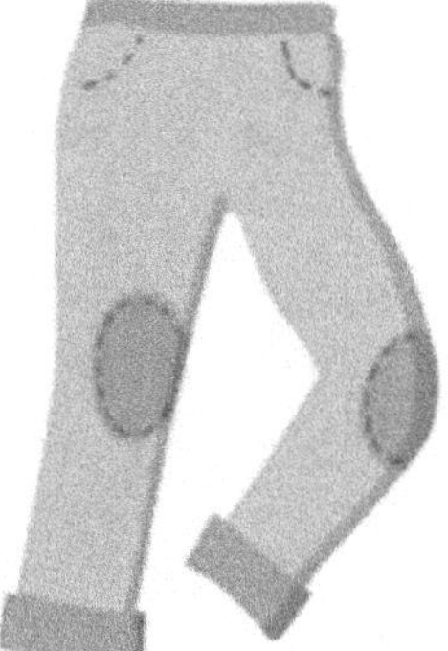

The trousers look like jeans.

slip

תַחתוֹנִים

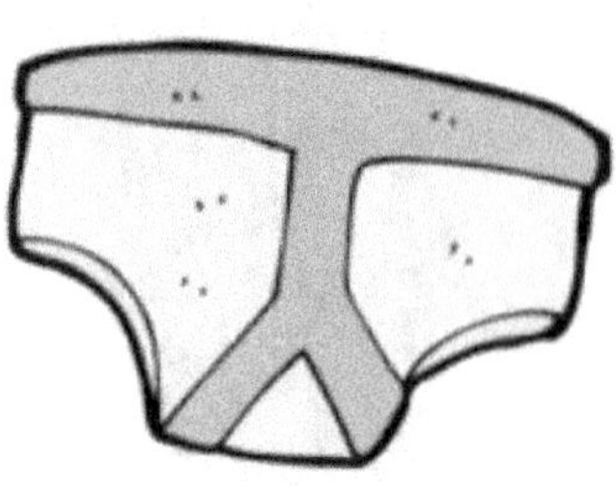

I always wear my underwear.

maillot de corps

My undershirt has a star.

une

Number one and the bee are friends.

deux

The cat and the mouse both love two.

trois

The bear gives number three a present.

quatre

Number four is a home for the cat.

cinq

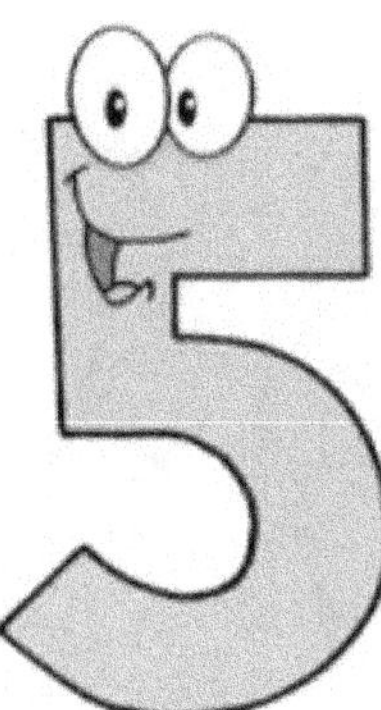

Number five hatches an egg.

six

שֵׁשׁ

Number six is going to eat a carrot.

sept

שֶׁבַע

Number seven is playing with the tiger.

huit

שְׁמוֹנֶה

Number eight is funny.

neuf

תֵּשַׁע

Number nine meets the parrot.

dix

עֶשֶׂר

Number ten is smiling.

onze

אַחַד עָשָׂר

Number eleven has big eyes.

douze

שתיים עשרה

Number twelve is number one and two.

treize

שְׁלוֹש עֶשְׂרֵה

Number thirteen is excited.

quatorze

ארבעה עשר

The number fourteen is vast.

quinze

חֲמֵשׁ עֶשְׂרֵה

The number fifteen is green.

seize

שש עשרה

Sixteen is my lucky number.

dix-sept

שבע עשרה

Number seventeen look alike.

dix-huit

שמונה עשרה

Number eighteen will go to the circus.

dix-neuf

תשע עשרה

I am nineteen now!

vingt

עשרים

Number twenty has a zero.

fourmi

נְמָלָה

The ant has lots of legs.

cloche

פַּעֲמוֹן

The bell will ring.

vache

פָּרָה

The cow has a bow.

poupée

בּוּבָּה

She has a cute bear doll.

oeuf

בֵּיצָה

The chick has hatched out of the egg.

poisson

דָג

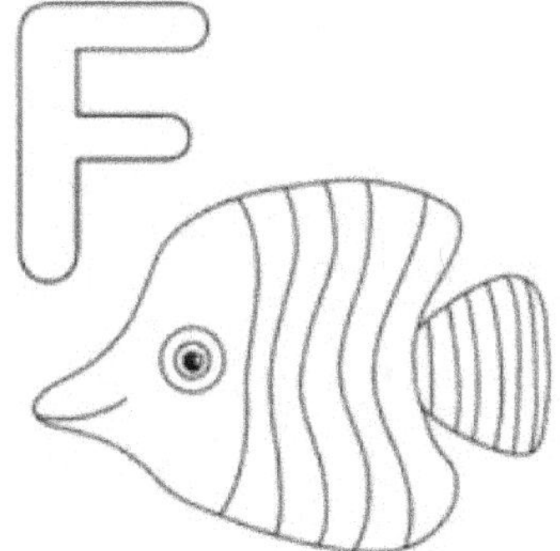

The fish is swimming in the water.

chèvre

עֵז

The goat is sitting on the grass.

chapeau

כּוֹבַע

He is wearing a hat.

crème glacée

גלידה

I like to eat ice cream.

confiture

The kitten is sitting on the jam jar.

chaton

The cat is sleeping on the floor.

lion

The lion is waiting for the tiger.

rat

The mouse has lots of presents.

nez

The reindeer has a red nose.

hibou

The owl is sleeping.

porc

חֲזִיר

The pig will eat cupcakes.

reine

מַלְכָּה

The queen has a big crown.

lapin

אַרְנָב

The rabbit is jumping up and down.

mouton

כבשים

The sheep have fluffy wool.

tortue

צָב

The turtle has a shell.

parapluie

מְטְרִיָה

The mouse is holding an umbrella.

van

ואן

The van is driving along the road.

pastèque

אבטיח

The watermelon has lots of seeds.

xylophone

קְסִילוֹפוֹן

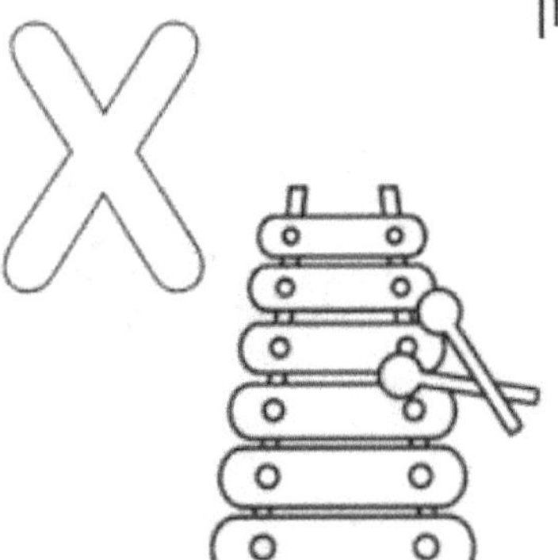

We are going to play the xylophone.

yaourt

יוגורט

We opened the yogurt can.

zèbre

זֶבְּרָה

The zebra is surprised.

rose

וָרוֹד

color the word and
the picture in pink

Most of my clothes are pink.

marron

חום

color the word and
the picture in pink

My chocolate is brown.

gris

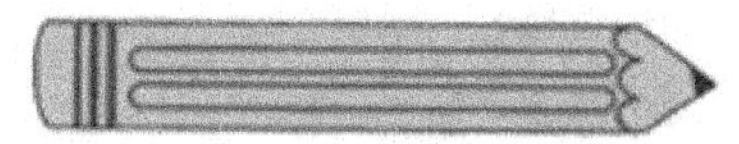

אפור

color the word and
the picture in pink

I don't like the color gray.

vert

ירוק

color the word and
the picture in pink

The vegetables are green.

jaune

צהוב

color the word and
the picture in pink

Bananas are yellow.

blanc

לבן

color the word and
the picture in pink

The paper that I write on is white.

rouge

אָדוֹם

color the word and
the picture in pink

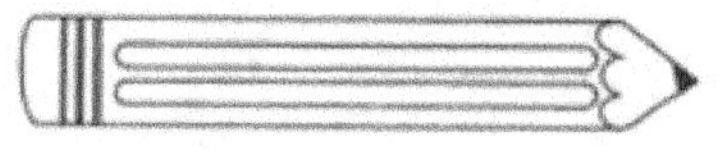

Apples are red.

bleu

כָּחֹל

The night sky is blue.

percer

תרגיל

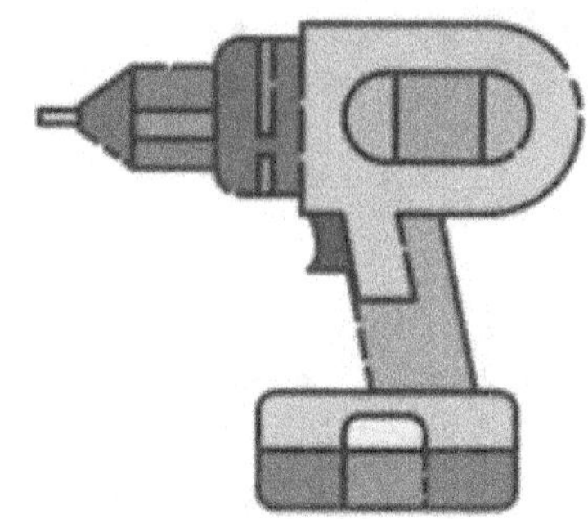

The drill will help us fix this.

marteau

פטיש

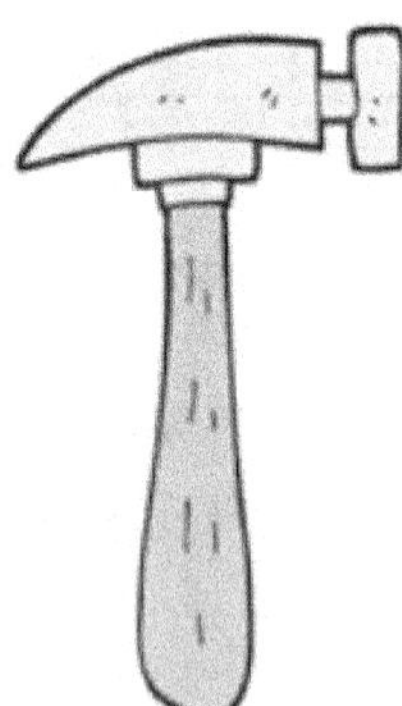

The hammer is going to nail the picture.

couteau

סַכִּין

The knife is sharp.

pinces

צְבָת

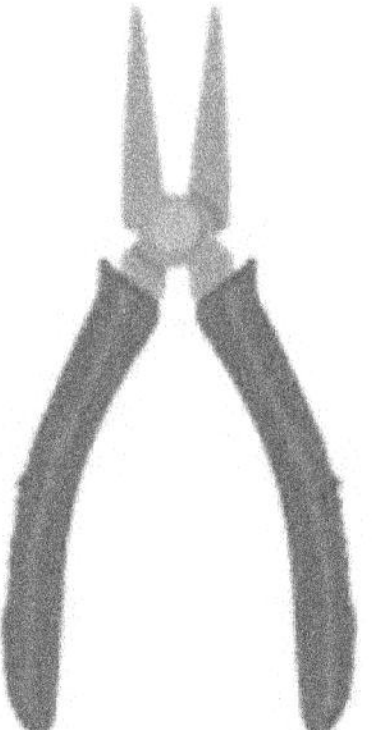

The plier is used for many things.

vu

ראה

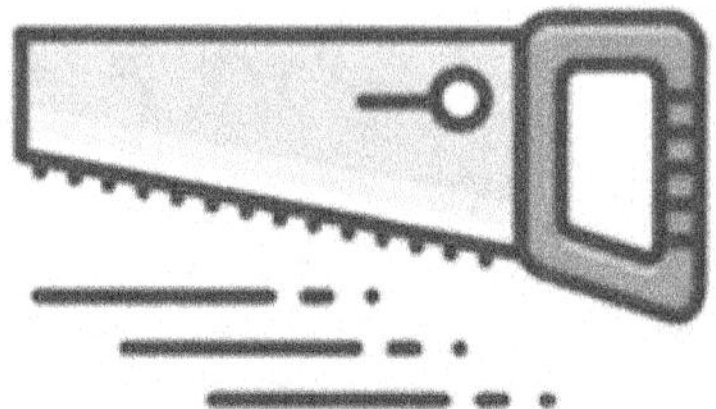

The saw can chop wood.

les ciseaux

מספריים

I use scissors to cut paper.

tournevis

מברג

The screwdriver can screw in the knots.

clé

מפתח ברגים

The wrench can help unscrew the knots.

avion

מטוס

The airplane is going to leave now.

vélo

אופניים

The bicycle is beautiful.

bateau

סִירָה

The boat is floating on the water.

autobus

אוֹטוֹבּוּס

The bus is going to school.

voiture

אוֹטוֹ

The car is green.

hélicoptère

מָסוֹק

The helicopter is looking for something.

cheval

סוּס

You can ride the horse.

jet

מטוס סילון

The jet is high-speed.

moto

אוֹפנוֹע

The motorcycle is on the road.

The ship is on the water.

My mom goes on the subway to work.

The taxi has someone inside.

The train is going slowly.

The truck has stuff in it.

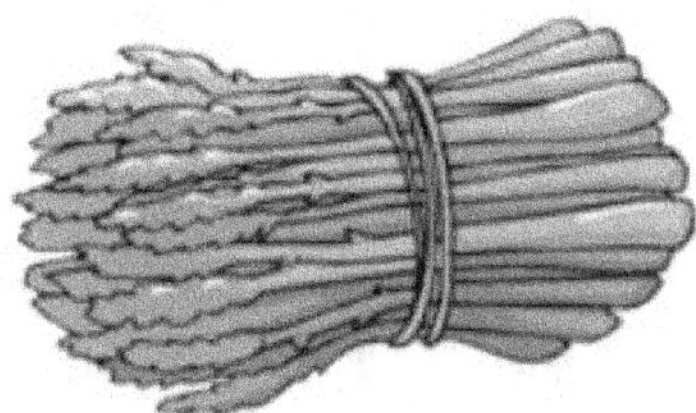

The asparagus is in a bundle.

des haricots

שעועית

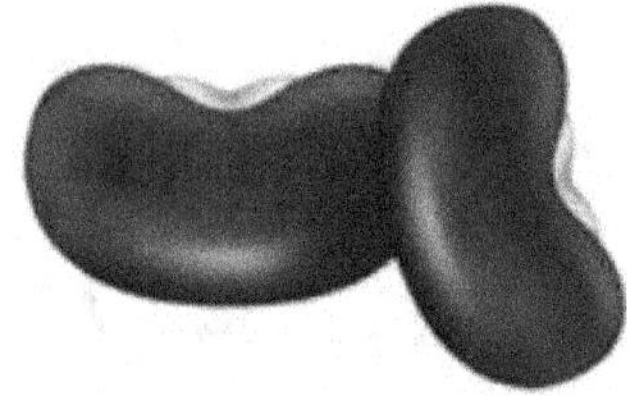

The beans are smooth.

brocoli

ברוקולי

The broccoli is dancing.

chou

כרוב

Bunnies like to eat cabbage.

carotte

גזר

The carrots are very long.

céleri

סלרי

The celery has lots of leaves.

blé

תירס

Corn soup is delicious.

concombre

מלפפון

The cucumbers are cut into pieces.

aubergine

חציל

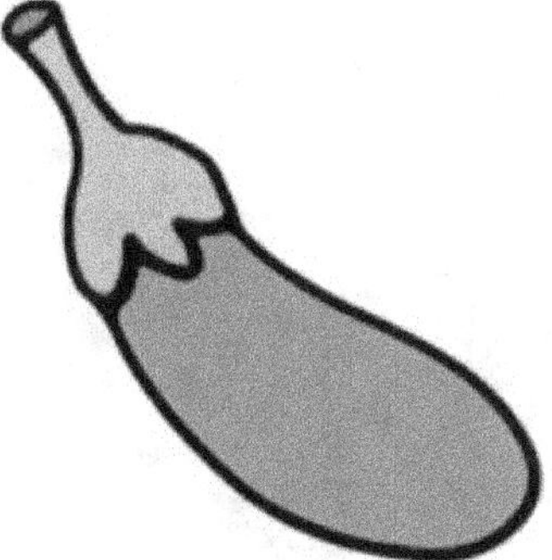

The eggplant is purple.

poivre vert

פלפל ירוק

The green pepper is juicy.

salade

חסה

The lettuce is all green.

oignon

בצל

The onions make my eyes water.

pois

אפונה

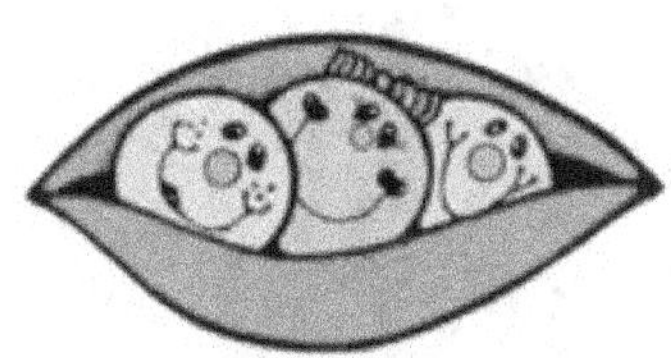

The peas are all in a pod.

patate

תפוח אדמה

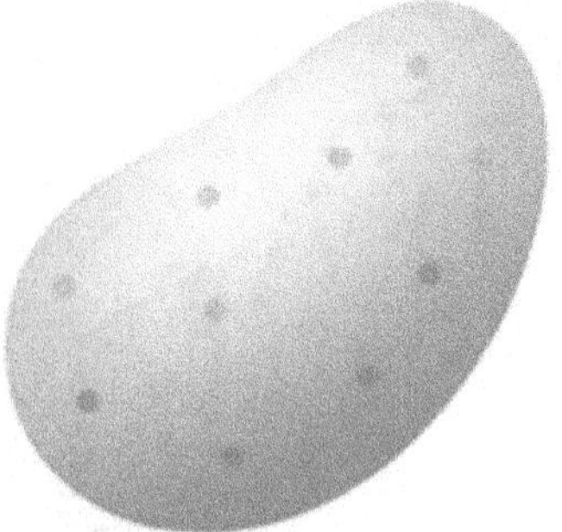

The potato is very shiny.

citrouille

דלעת

The pumpkin is for Halloween.

un radis

צְנוֹן

The radish is a type of vegetable.

épinard

תרד

The spinach is good with cheese.

patate douce

בטטה

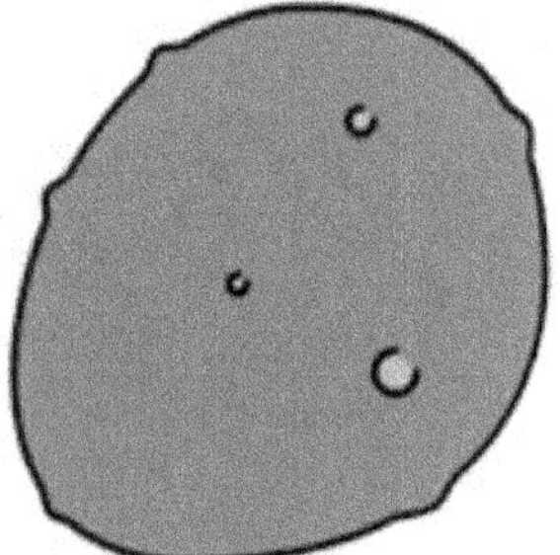

The sweet potato is quite sweet.

tomate

עגבנייה

I don't like to eat tomatoes.

navet

לפת

My mom bought some turnips.

nuageux

מְעוּנָן

The weather is cloudy today.

du froid

קַר

I like cold weather.

cool

קָרִיר

The temperature is cold today.

brumeux

מעורפל

The fog is so strong I can't see the city.

chaud

חַם

The fire is burning hot.

humide

לַח

It's so humid and wet today.

pluvieux

גָּשׁוּם

It's raining very hard.

neigeux

מוּשְׁלָג

Welcome to snow land!

orageux

סוֹעֵר

I hate the stormy weather.

ensoleillé

שִׁמְשִׁי

The sun is shining!

chaud

נָעִים

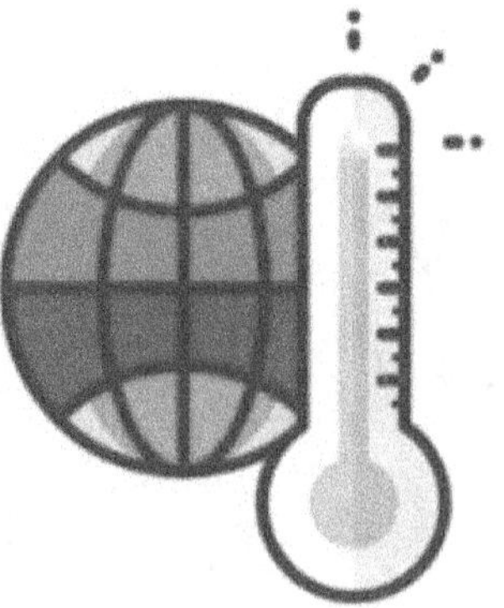

The whole world is warm today!

venteux

סוֹעֵר

The leaves are blowing away since it's so windy!

tante

דּוֹדָה

My aunt is very nice to me.

frère

אָח

My brother is very fun to play with.

cousin

בת דודה

I love going to the playground with my cousin.

fille

בַּת

I like to read books with my daughter.

père

אַבָּא

My father is playing with me.

petite fille

נֶכְדָה

My granddaughter has blond hair.

grand-mère

סַבְתָא

My grandmother is very old and has glasses.

petit fils

נֶכֶד

My grandson and I are very excited today!

mère

אִמָא

My mother likes to pick me up.

neveu

אחיין

My father's nephew is my cousin.

nièce

אחיינית

My niece is very good at playing ball.

sœur

אָחוֹת

My sister is so pretty!

fils

בֵּן

My son likes to play with toy cars.

belle fille

בת חורגת

My stepdaughter likes the color orange.

belle-mère

אמא חורגת

My stepmother is pretty.

beau-fils

בֵּן חוֹרֵג

This is my stepson, Greg.

oncle

דוד

My uncle tells lots of funny jokes.

bol

קְעָרָה

The bowl has nothing inside.

tasse

גָּבִיעַ

My mom drinks her coffee out of a cup.

plat

צַלַּחַת

That dish has a bone inside.

fourchette

מזלג

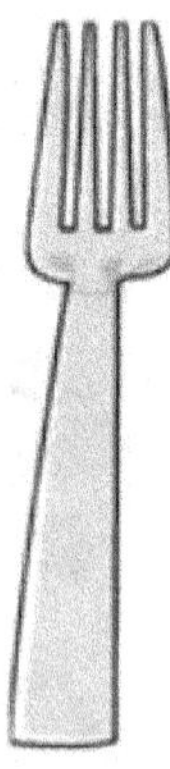

We have more spoons than forks.

verre

זכוכית

I have a glass of water on my desk.

couteau

סַכִּין

I have a knife in my kitchen.

agresser

ספל

This mug of coffee is for my dad.

serviette de table

מַפִּית

You can use the napkins to clean your hands.

poivre

פלפל

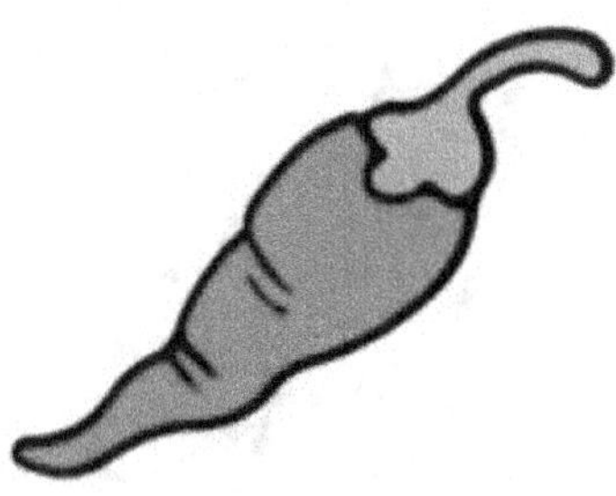

The pepper is very spicy.

lanceur

כַּד

Pour yourself some lemonade from the pitcher.

assiette

צַלַחַת

Can you help me wash the plates?

salade

סלט

The salad is very healthy for you.

sel

מלח

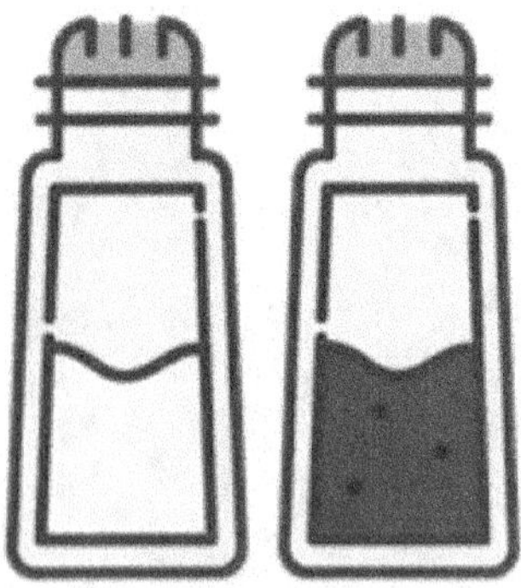

The salt tastes good with a few pinches of pepper.

soucoupe

צַלַחַת

The plate is for my cup.

cuillère

כף

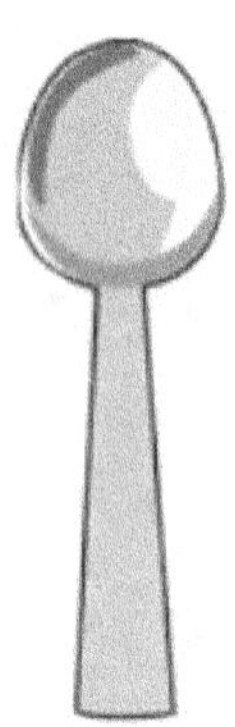

I use a spoon to eat my rice.

sucre

סוכר

The pack of sugar is very heavy.

dimanche

יום ראשון

Sunday

Sunday is the day to go to Church!

lundi

יוֹם שֵׁנִי

Monday

Monday is the day to start school.

mardi

יוֹם שְׁלִישִׁי

Tuesday

We will go to the shops on Tuesday.

mercredi

יום רביעי

Wednesday

Wednesday is hard to spell!

jeudi

יוֹם חֲמִישִׁי

Thursday

Thursday is the fourth day of the week!

vendredi

יוֹם שִׁישִׁי

Friday

My birthday is on Friday!

samedi

יום שבת

Saturday

Saturday is the weekend!

cuire

לֶאֱפוֹת

The chef will bake a cake.

ébullition

רְתִיחָה

I will boil the eggs.

griller

לְצָלוֹת

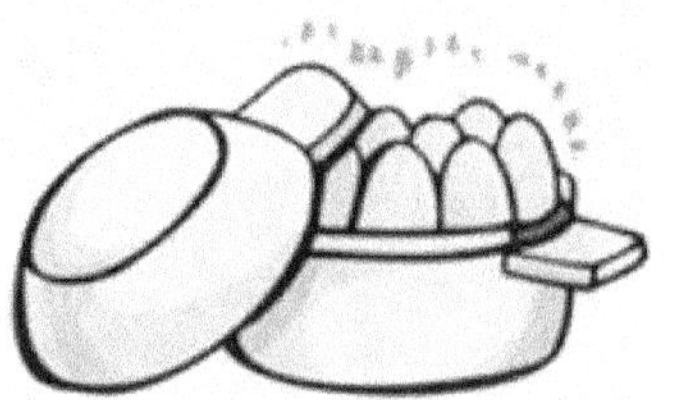

Broil is very yummy.

ouvre-boîte

פותחן

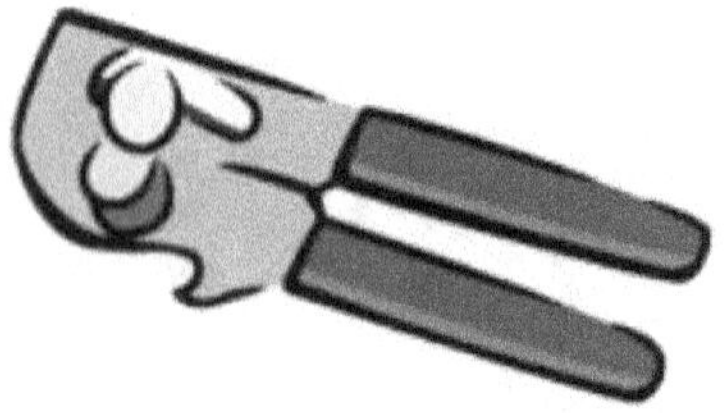

That can opener is used for
opening cans.

frire

לטגן

The pan can fry lots of things.

gril

גְרִיל

We have a grill in our backyard.

tasse à mesurer

כוס מדידה

My mom uses the measuring cup
for baking.

cuillère à mesurer

כף מדידה

I use a measuring spoon to eat my dessert.

four micro onde

מיקרוגל

The microwave is used to heat food.

bol à mélanger

קערת ערבוב

She is using the mixing bowl to mix things.

serviettes en papier

מגבות נייר

Dry your hands with paper towels.

poché aux œufs

צid ביצה

The poach is put on noodles.

porte pot

בעל סיר

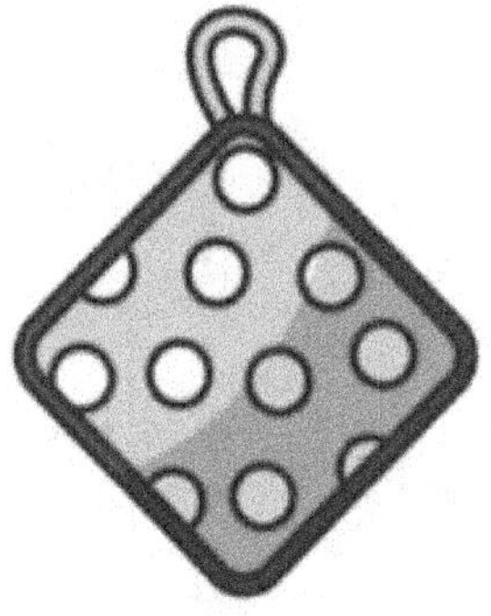

The potholder is soft.

rôti

צֶלִי

The chef made roast chicken.

rouleau à pâtisserie

מערוך

He is holding a rolling pin.

brouiller

לִטְרוֹף

My mom is making scrambled
eggs for breakfast.

mijoter

רְתִיחָה

The simmer is rice today.

couteau

סַכִּין

The knife is sharp.

cuillère

כף

I eat my food with a spoon and
fork.

spatule

מָרִית

The spatula will help us flip the steak over.

vapeur

קִיטוֹר

The steam is coming from the pot.

passoire

מְסַנֶּנֶת

The strainer is used to strain stuff.

minuteur

שָׁעוֹן עֶצֶר

I set my timer for 12:00.

fourchette

מזלג

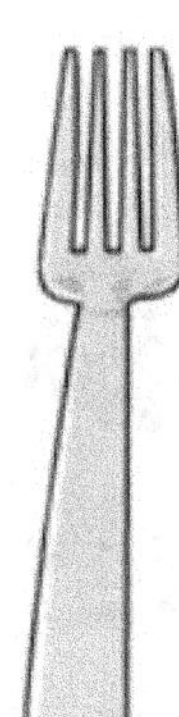

I have lots of metallic forks.

grille-pain

טוֹסְטֶר

The toaster will toast my bread.

bouilloire

קוּמְקוּם

The kettle has tea inside.

réfrigérateur

מְקָרֵר

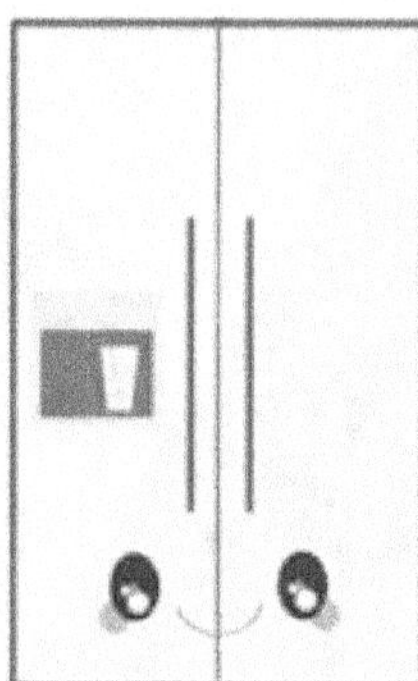

The refrigerator has lots of things inside.

mixeur

מַמְחֶה

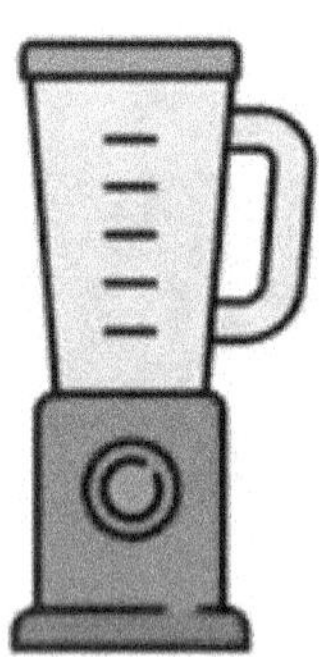

The blender will mix up my fruits.

cabinets

ארונות

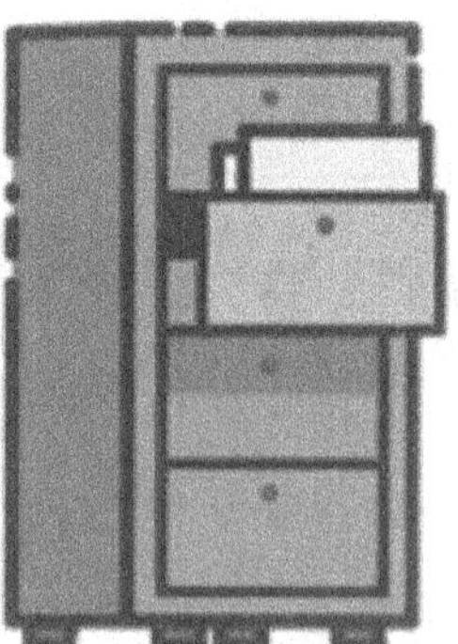

The cabinet has my paper inside.

placard

אָרוֹן

The cupboard has lots of books.

four micro onde

מיקרוגל

The microwave will heat my food.

arrière

חזור

She has a slender back.

des joues

לחיים

She kisses her mom on the cheek.

poitrine

חזה

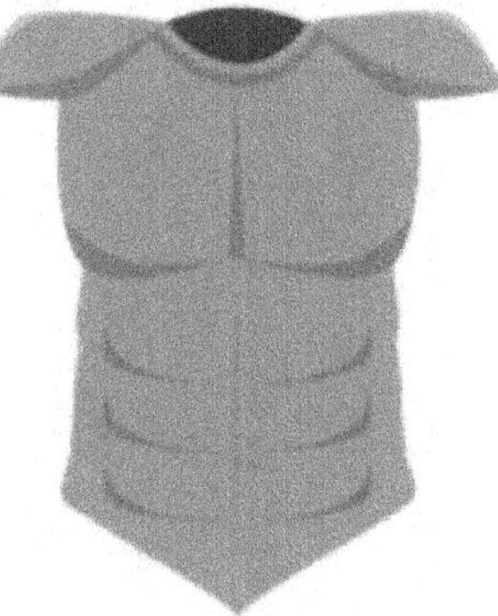

The armor is for your chest.

menton

סַנְטֵר

This is my chin!

oreilles

אוזניים

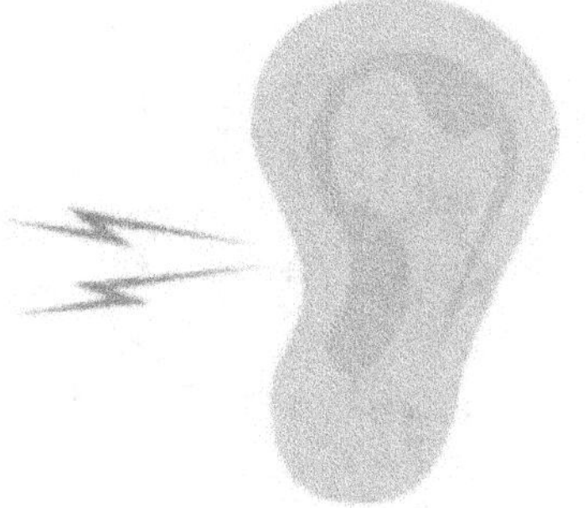

The ear is hearing something.

les sourcils

גבות

The eyebrows are raised.

yeux

עיניים

The eyes are blue.

pieds

רגליים

I have one pair of feet.

des doigts

אצבעות

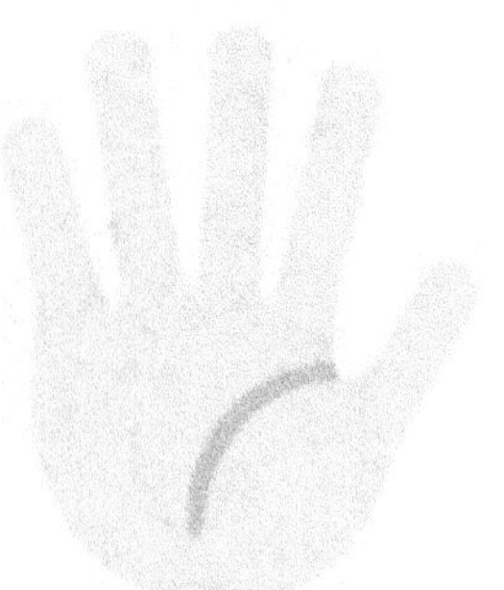

The fingers are waving at us.

pied

כף רגל

My foot has five fingers.

front

מצח

My brain is behind my forehead.

cheveux

שיער

My hair is long and black.

mains

ידיים

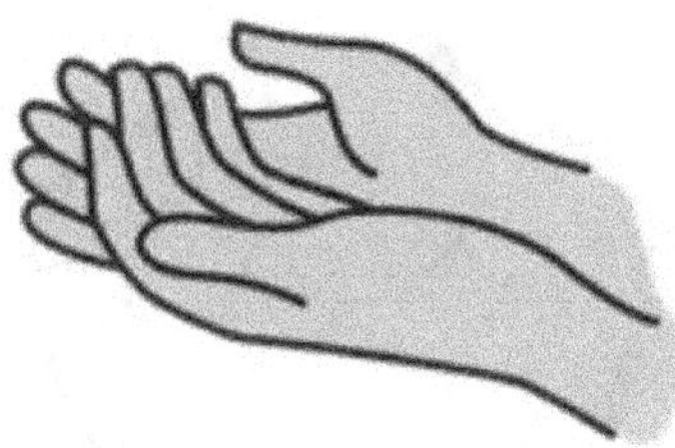

I will wash my hands in the sink.

tête

רֹאשׁ

She has a big head.

les hanches

מָתְנַיִם

The gorilla has his hands on his hips.

les genoux

ברכיים

She is begging on her knees.

jambes

רגליים

The tiger has strong legs.

lèvres

שפתיים

The lips have lipstick on.

bouche

פֶּה

He is covering his mouth with his hand.

cou

צוואר

The necklace is very special to me.

nez

אַף

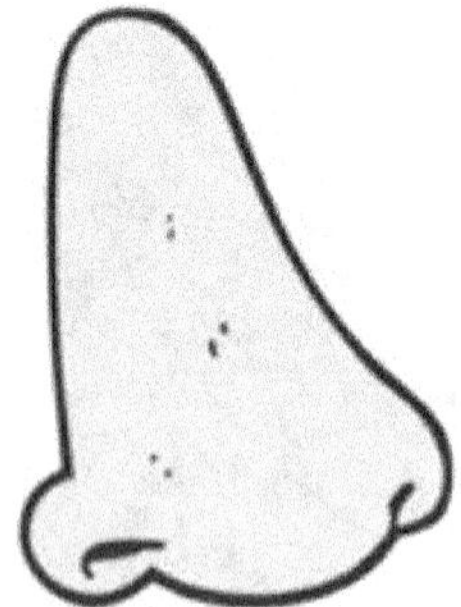

The nose smells something.

épaules

כתפיים

He puts his hands on his shoulders.

estomac

בֶּטֶן

He has a big stomach.

les dents

שיניים

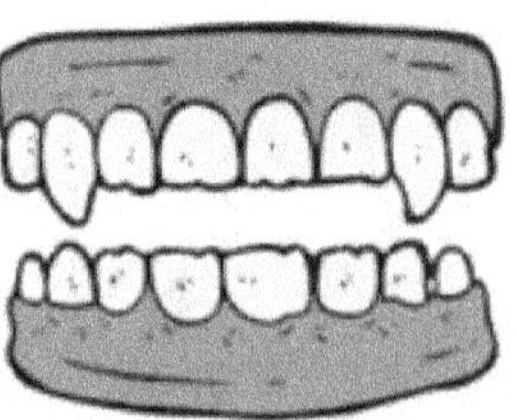

The teeth are clean and white.

gorge

גרון

He has a sore throat today.

les orteils

אצבעות רגליים

My toes are small.

langue

לָשׁוֹן

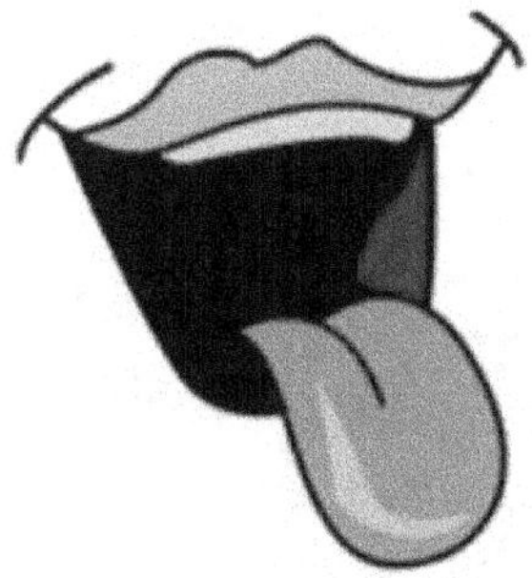

My tongue is licking ice cream.

dent

שֵׁן

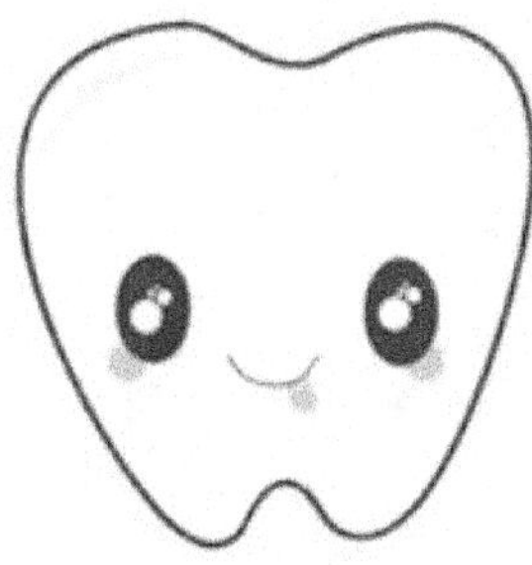

The tooth has big eyes.

taille

מׇתְנַיִם

He has his hands on his waist.

salopette

סרבלים

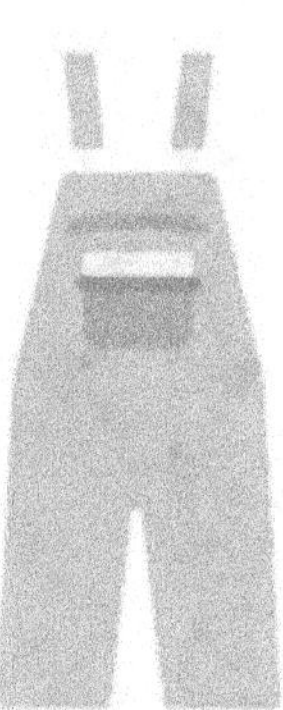

I bought these overalls for you!

mitaines

כְּסָיוֹת

The mittens are very warm.

bonnet

כִּפָּה

The beanie is for winter.

tablier

סִינָר

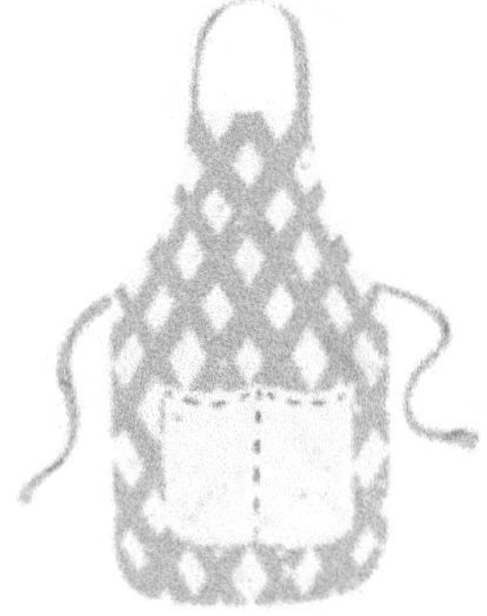

I wear my apron when I bake.

poupée

בּוּבָּה

The doll is for my baby sister.

hochets

רַעֲשָׁנִים

The rattle is for the baby.

jouet

צַעֲצוּעַ

The toy is very fun.

couche

לְחַתֵּל

The baby has to wear a diaper.

berceau

באסינט

She is sleeping in her bassinet.

bavoir

בִּיב

My baby brother has to wear his
bib when he is eating.

octogone

מְתוּמָן

The octagon is saying okay!

triangle

משולש

The triangle has three corners.

carré

כיכר

Squxare

The square has four sides.

cercle

Circle

The circle is round.

ovale

The oval shape looks like a circle.

cœur

I drew a heart on my paper.

traverser

That sign is a cross.

la flèche

The arrow is pointing this way.

cube

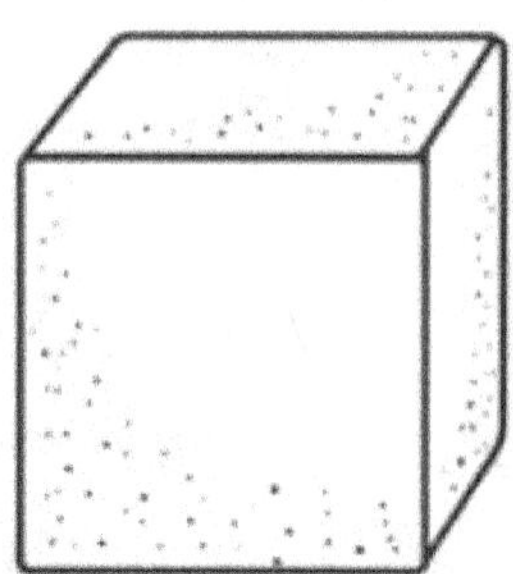

The cube is 3D.

étoile

כוכב

The star is yellow and shiny.

tir à l'arc

קַשתֻות

The archery is where you aim.

badminton

נוצית

My favorite sport is badminton.

criquet

קרִיקֶט

I am very good at cricket.

bowling

בָּאוּלִינג

I got one pin down at bowling!

boxe

אֶגרוּף

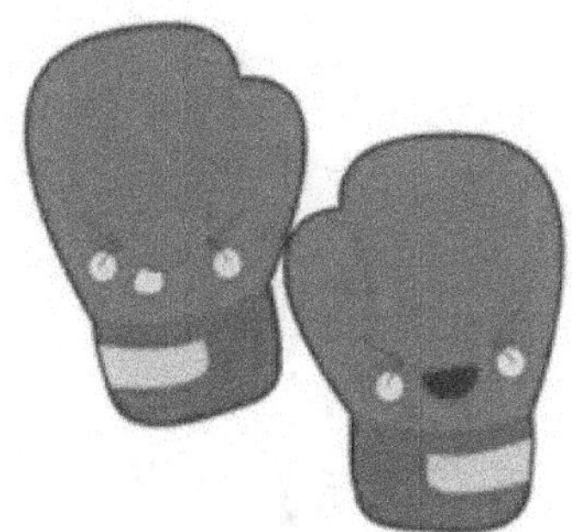

The boxing gloves are hot.

tennis

טֶנִיס

He can hit the ball in tennis.

faire de la planche a roulettes

רכיבה על סקייטבורד

He skateboards to school.

planche de surf

גלישת גלים

The shark loves surfing in the ocean.

le hockey

הוֹקֵי

I like to play Ice hockey.

yoga

יוֹגָה

He is closing his eyes and doing yoga.

épée

סִיּוּף

They are fencing and dueling together.

aptitude

She will do some fitness in the pool.

gymnastique

He can do brilliant gymnastics.

karaté

She is good at kicking in Karate.

volley-ball

She is holding a volleyball.

musculation

The girl with brown hair can do weightlifting.

basketball

He can balance the ball with one finger in basketball.

base-ball

בייסבול

The little chick is in the finales at baseball.

le rugby

רוגבי

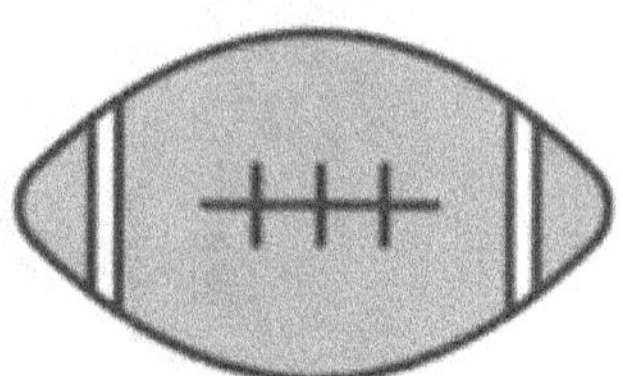

The rugby ball has white stripes.

lutte

הַאֲבְקוּת

The sumo will compete in wrestling.

course de voitures

מירוץ מכוניות

He is number one for car racing.

cyclisme

רכיבה על אופניים

He is peacefully cycling on the road.

fonctionnement

רץ

He is running while listening to his earphones.

tennis de table

טניס שולחן

My brother and dad will play table tennis.

pêche

דיג

He will go to the river to fish.

judo

ג'ודו

She has a red belt in Judo.

escalade

טיפוס

He will climb the ladder.

tournage

צילומים

He is shooting the archery board.

le golf

גולף

She is going to compete in the golf competition.

balade

נְסִיעָה

He will ride his scooter.

asseyez-vous

לָשֶׁבֶת

They are sitting down together.

se lever

תַעֲמוֹד

She likes to stand up.

bats toi

מַאֲבָק

They are fighting over the book.

rire

לִצְחוֹק

He is laughing so hard!

lis

לִקְרוֹא

She read a picture book.

jouer

לְשַׂחֵק

He went to play on the slide.

ecoutez

להקשיב

He listened for the ice cream cart.

pleurer

בוכה

He cried because he got a bad grade.

pense

לַחשוב

He thought that the test would be hard.

chanter

לָשִׁיר

He sang for the concert.

regarder la télévision

צופה בטלוויזיה

He watched TV the whole night.

danse

לִרְקוֹד

She was a good dancer.

allumer

להדליק

The light is turned on.

éteindre

לכבות

The light is turned off.

gagner

לנצח

He won the contest.

mouche

לטוס, זבוב

The parrot can fly.

couper

גזירה

He was cutting his nails.

désinvolte

לזרוק

He threw away the garbage.

dormir

לִישֹׁן

He slept soundly.

fermer

סגור

He closed his mouth shut.

ouvert

לִפְתוֹחַ

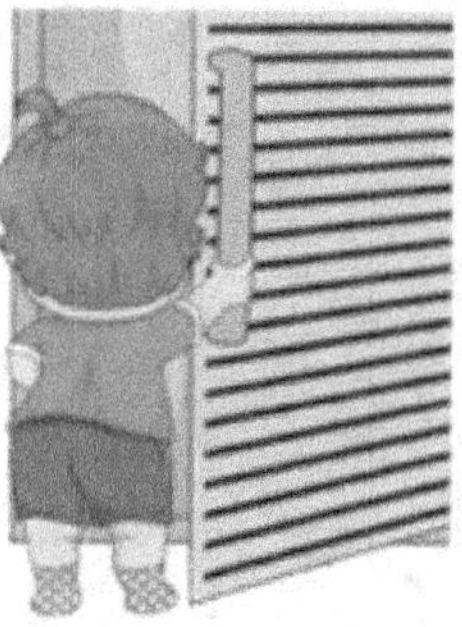

She opened the bathroom door.

écrire

לכתוב

She wrote with a pencil.

donner

לָתֵת

Santa gave her a present.

sauter

קְפִיצָה

She had fun jumping.

manger

לֶאֱכוֹל

The shark ate yummy ice cream.

boisson

לִשְׁתּוֹת

The old British man drank tea.

cuisinier

לְבַשֵׁל

The microwave cooked his soup.

lavage

לִשְׁטוֹף

You need to remember to wash
your hands.

attendre

לַחֲכוֹת

He was waiting for the bus.

montée

לְטַפֵּס

She climbed a lot of mountains.

parler

דבר

Two best friends were talking together.

crawl

לזחול

The baby crawled on the floor.

rêver

חולם

The Sloth dreamed about eating leaves.

creuser

לַחפּור

That strong man dug a swimming pool.

taper

לטפוֹחַ

The baby clapped her hands.

tricoter

לִסְרוֹג

She knits with the purple string.

coudre

לִתְפּוֹר

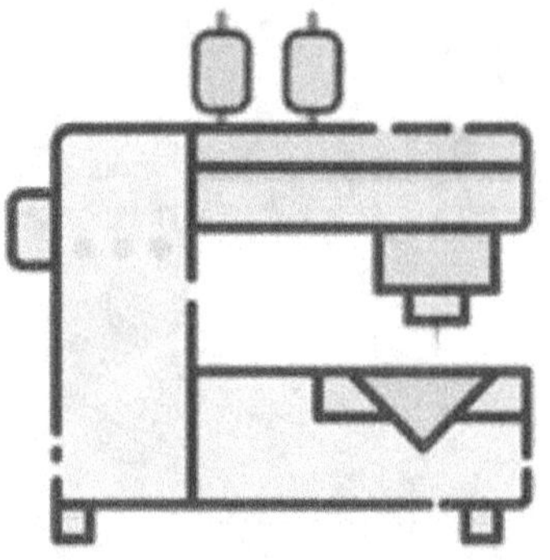

That is a sewing machine.

odeur

רֵיחַ

The perfume smelled great.

baiser

נְשִׁיקָה

He kissed his mother.

étreinte

לְחַבֵּק

They hugged each other.

ronfler

לִנְחוֹר

The tiger snored.

baigner

לִרְחוֹץ

He took a bath.

s'incliner

הַרכֵּנָה

He bowed to the judge.

peindre

צֶבַע

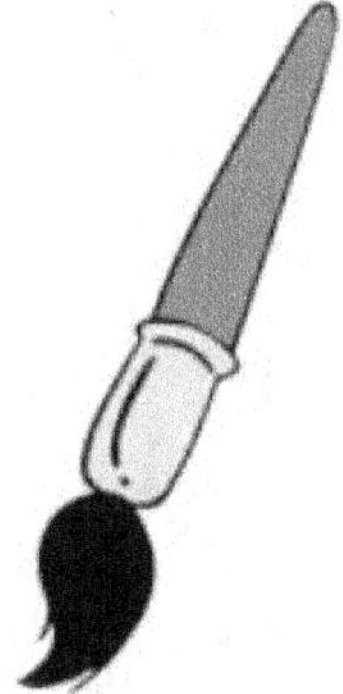

He painted a colorful picture.

se plonger

לִצְלוֹל

He dove to the deepest part of the ocean.

ski

סקִי

The ski was expensive.

empiler

לַעֲרוֹם

The books are stacked high.

acheter

לִקְנוֹת

They bought cereal.

secouer

לְנַעֵר

They shook hands together.

programmeur

מְתַכְנֵת

He was a smart computer programmer.

vétérinaire

וֶטֶרִינָר

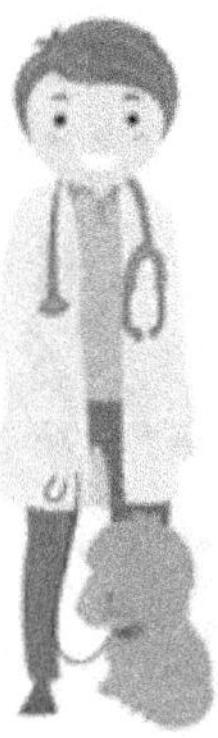

She is a veterinarian.

vendeur de rue

רוכל

That street vendor sells hot dogs.

mineur

כּוֹרֶה

That Miner will find gold.

prof

מוֹרֶה

The owl is the teacher.

groom

בלוי

That Bellboy is fat.

orateur

רַמקוֹל

The chicken is a great Speaker.

boucher

קַצָּב

The Butcher sells fish.

pharmacien

רוֹקֵחַ

That Pharmacist saved a person's life.

réceptionniste

פְּקִיד קַבָּלָה

He is a Receptionist.

politicien

פּוֹלִיטִיקָאִי

He wants to be a Politician.

guide touristique

מדריך טיולים

That Tour guide led us around Japan.

entrepreneur

יזם

He is an Entrepreneur.

danseuse de ballet

רקדן בלט

She is training to be a Ballet dancer.

astronaute

אַסטרוֹנָאוּט

He is a great astronaut.

juge

לִשְׁפּוֹט

That Judge is always fair.

avocat

עורך דין

The lawyer is serious.

la caissière

קופאית

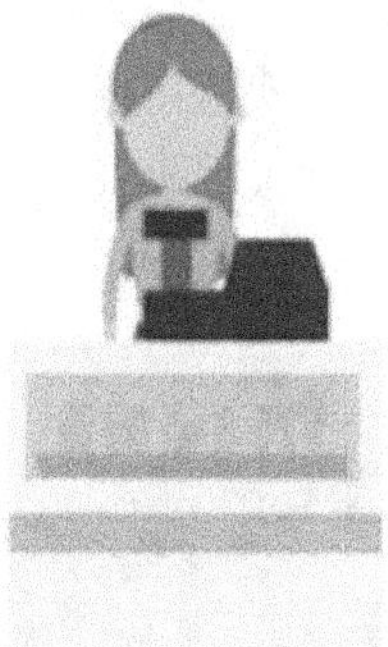

She is a cashier at the market.

conducteur de taxi

נהג מונית

He is a fast Taxi driver.

plombier

שרברב

That Plumber fixes toilets.

musicien

מוּסִיקָאִי

She wants to be a Musician like her teacher.

chef

שֶׁף

The chef makes fast food.

boulanger

אוֹפֶה

That baker is a bread.

artiste

אמן

That Artist came from Italy.

acteur

שַׂחְקָן

That actor is famous.

barman

ברמן

The Bartender works in a bar.

coiffeur

מעצבת שיער

That girl is a Hairdresser.

évêques

בישופים

He is a Bishop.

opticien

אוֹפְּטִיקָאִי

She went to an Optician.

fleuriste

מוֹכֵר פְּרָחִים

She is a great Florist.

écrivain

סוֹפֵר

He is a famous author.

comptable

רואת חשבון

My accountant is loyal.

du vin

יַיִן

That wine tastes good.

café

קפה

That coffee is bitter.

limonade

לימונדה

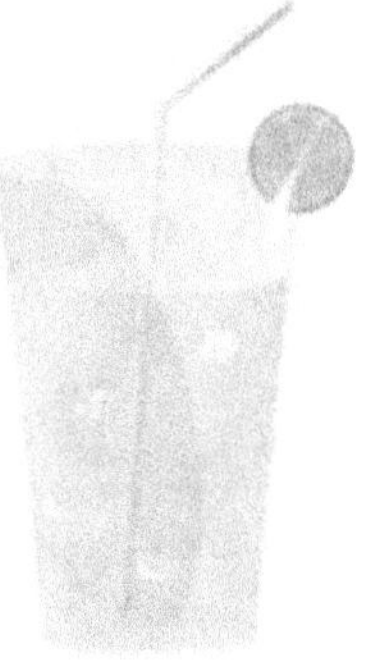

The lemonade is refreshing.

chocolat chaud

שוקו חם

I drink hot chocolate every day.

milk-shake

מילקשייק

The milkshake has whipped cream.

eau

מים

The water is not cold.

thé

תה

The tea is hot.

lait

חלב

Milk is white.

bière

בירה

The beer is foamy.

un soda

סודה

The soda is fizzy.

smoothie

אָדָם חֲלַקְלַק

The smoothie is a watermelon flavor.

milk-shake

מילקשייק

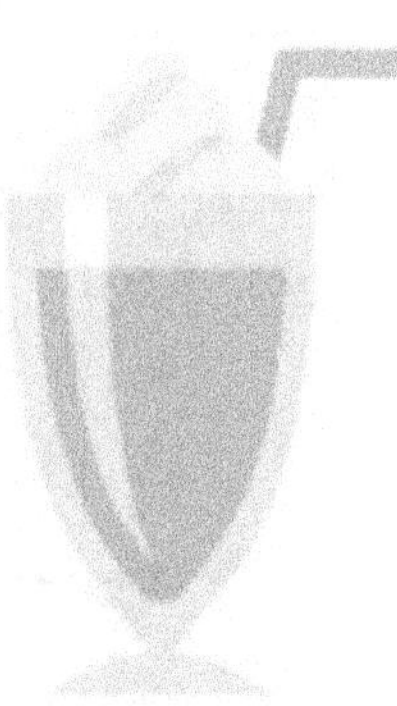

The milkshake has whipped cream.

lait de coco

חלב קוקוס

The coconut milk is yummy.

du jus d'orange

מיץ תפוזים

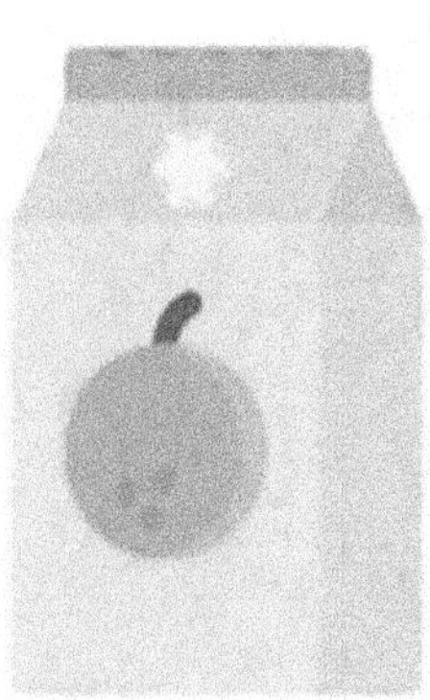

The orange juice is made from oranges.

cacao

קקאו

The cocoa is sweet.

fromage

גבינה

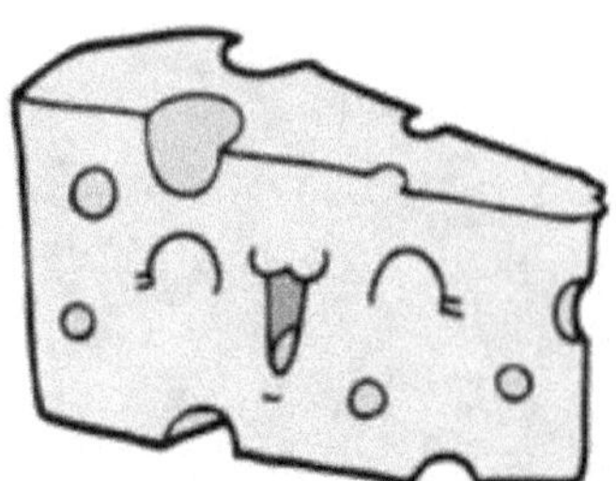

The cheese is creamy.

oeuf

ביצה

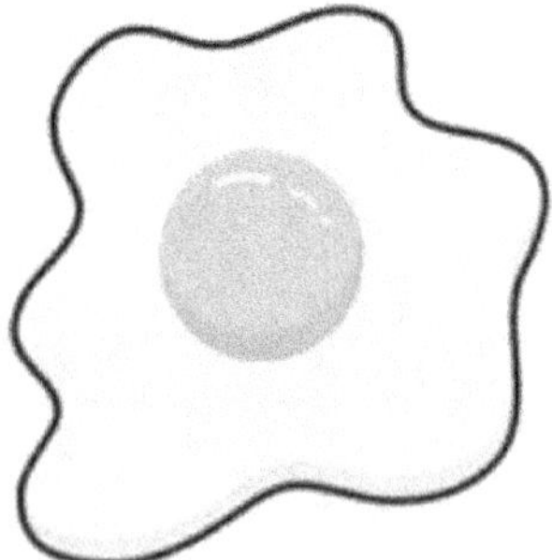

The egg is fried.

beurre

חמאה

The butter is put on bread.

margarine

מרגרינה

Margarine looks like butter.

yaourt

יוגורט

That yogurt is popular.

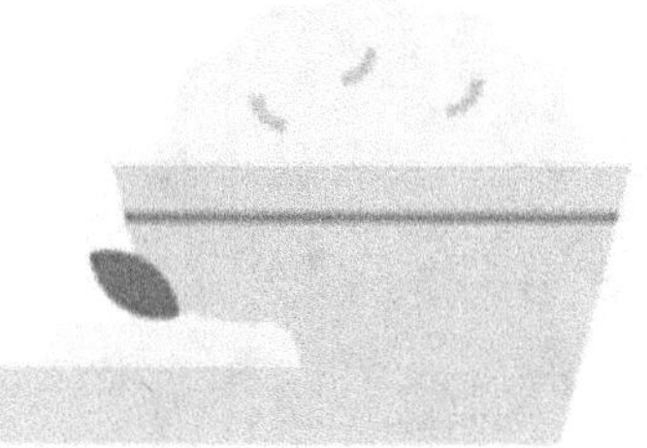

The cottage cheese is put on crackers.

They have a triple scoop ice cream.

That is a lot of creams.

That sandwich is healthy.

Americans love sausages.

That hamburger looks happy.

hot-dog

נקניקיה

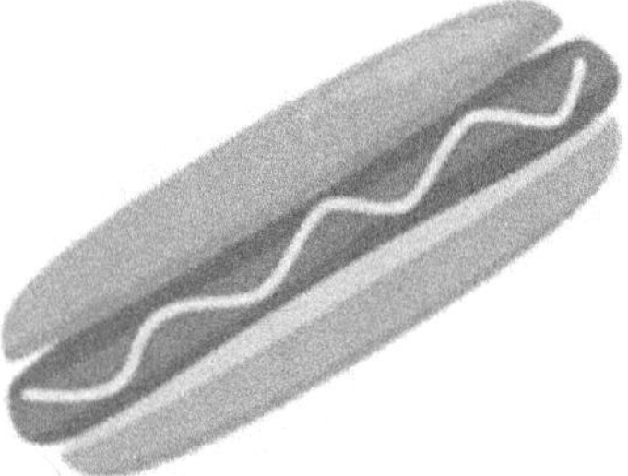

That hot dog has mustard on it.

pain

לחם

That bread is saying hello.

pizza

פיצה

That pizza is cheesy.

steak

סטייק

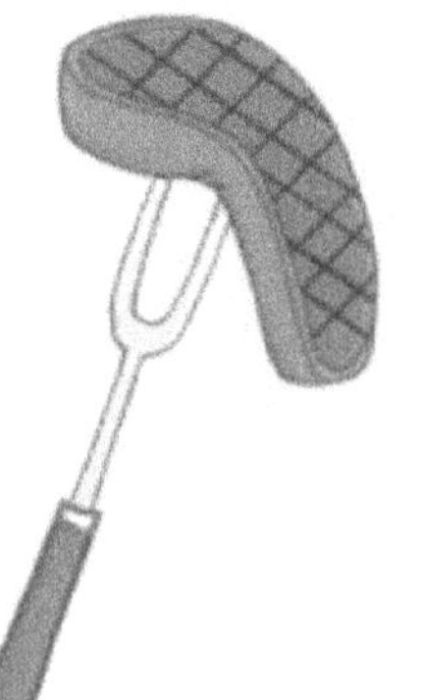

The steak was grilled.

poulet rôti

תרנגול צלוי

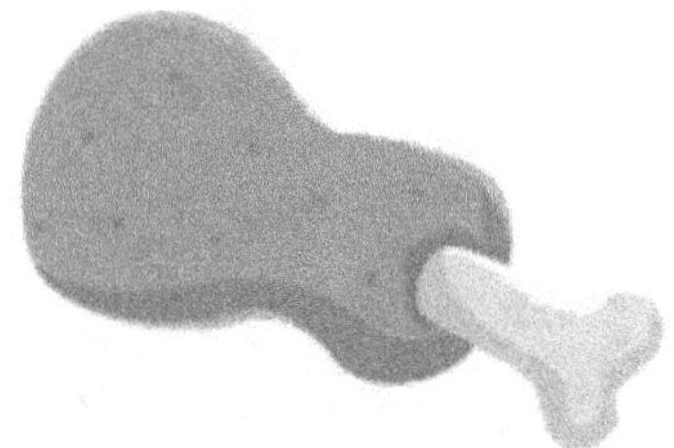

Roast Chicken is delicious.

poisson

דג

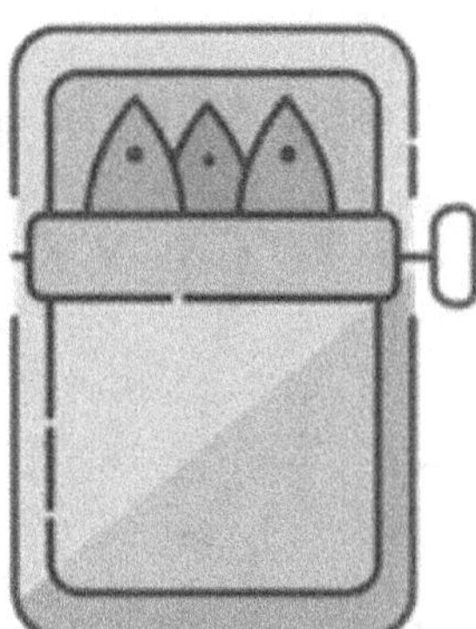

You can buy canned fish in the market.

fruit de mer

פירות ים

Lobster is expensive seafood.

jambon

חזיר

Ham can be put in sandwiches.

kebab

קַבָּב

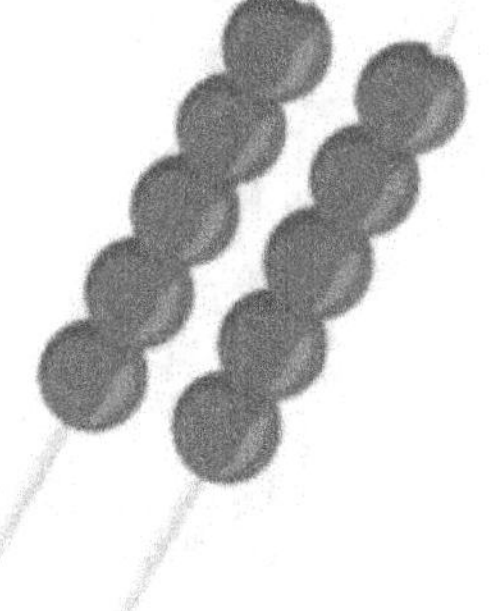

Kebab is a delicacy in America.

bacon

בייקון

That bacon is smiling.

crème fraîche

שמנת חמוצה

You can dip your chips in sour cream.

vache

פָּרָה

Cows are black and white.

lapin

ארנב

That rabbit is fun to play with.

canard

ברווז

That duck is content.

crevette

שרימפ

The shrimp has six legs.

porc

חֲזִיר

That pig is pink and fat.

abeille

דבורה

The bee has a stinger.

chèvre

עֵז

That goat has a white horn.

crabe

סרטן

The crab has two big pincers.

cerf

צְבִי

That deer is sleeping.

dinde

טורקיה

The turkey has a giant tail.

colombe

יוֹנָה

That dove is carrying a plant.

mouton

כבשים

That sheep has fluffy wool.

poisson

דג

That fish has colorful fins.

poulet

עוֹף

That chicken is waking everybody up.

cheval

סוּס

The horse has a red mane.

chaise

כִּסֵא

That wing chair is yellow.

meuble tv

מעמד טלוויזיה

The TV stand can hold books.

canapé

סַפָּה

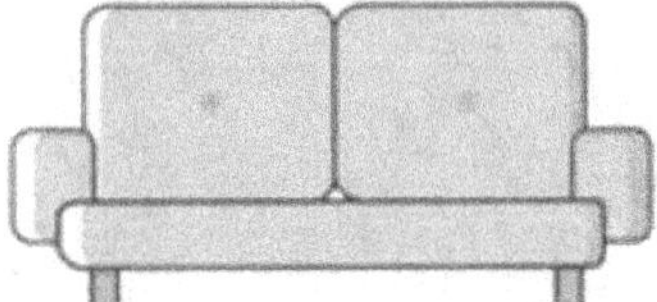

The sofa is comfortable to sit on.

coussins

כריות

The cushion helps soften your seat.

téléphone

טֶלֶפוֹן

The telephone is ringing.

télévision

טֶלֶוִיזְיָה

That television is big.

haut-parleurs

רמקולים

That speaker is used to increase the volume.

table d'appoint

שולחן צדדי

That end table is sparkling clean.

service à thé

סט תה

That tea set is from China.

cheminée

אָח

The fireplace makes me warm.

télécommandes

מרחוק

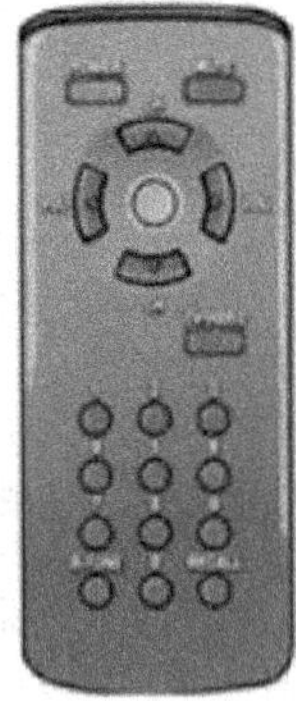

The remote has lots of buttons.

ventilateur électrique

מאוורר חשמלי

The fan is blowing wind.

lampadaire

מנורת רצפה

The floor lamp is very tall.

tapis

שָׁטִיחַ

The carpet is soft and silky.

bureaux

שולחנות עבודה

The table is made of wood.

stores

תריסים

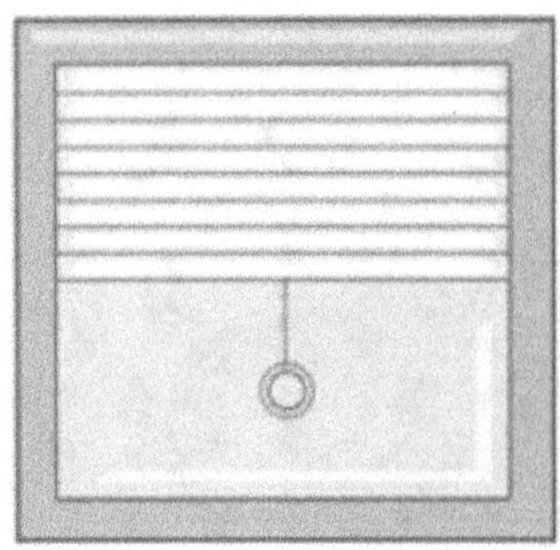

I will pull the blinds down.

rideaux

וילונות

She opened the curtains.

image

תְּמוּנָה

The picture is about the mountains and the sky.

vase

אֲגַרְטֵל

The roses are all in a vase.

l'horloge

שָׁעוֹן

The alarm clock is beeping.

oreiller

כרית

The pillow is pink and yellow.

cintre

קולב כובע

The hat stand has only one hat on it.

mettre la table

שולחן איפור

I have made up on my dressing table.

lampe de table

מנורת שולחן

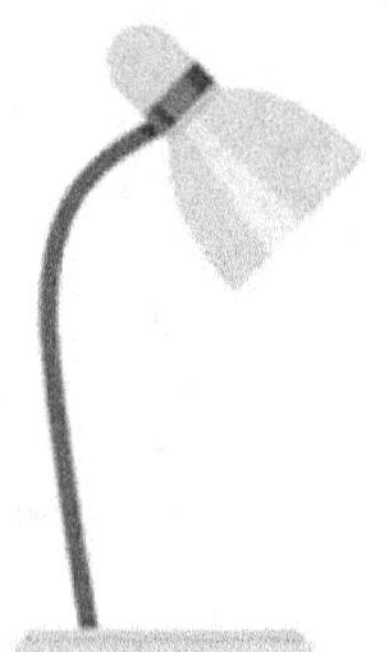

The table lamp will help me see in the dark.

miroir

מַרְאָה

The mirror is very tall.

planche a repasser

קרש גיהוץ

Don't touch the ironing board, it's hot!

boîte avec tiroir

תיבה עם מגירה

You can keep your clothes in the hope chest.

table de chevet

ארונית

The nightstand has my lamp on it.

lit

מיטה

The bed is charming.

climatisation

מזגן

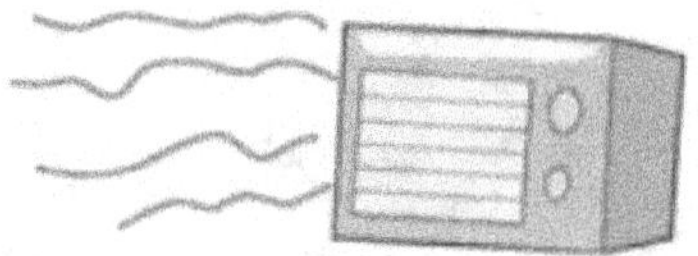

The air conditioner is cold.

cruche

כד

The measuring jug has nothing inside.

dentifrice

משחת שיניים

The toothpaste is mint flavored.

brosse à dents

מִברֶשֶׁת שִׁנַיִם

The toothbrush has toothpaste on it.

savon

סַבּוֹן

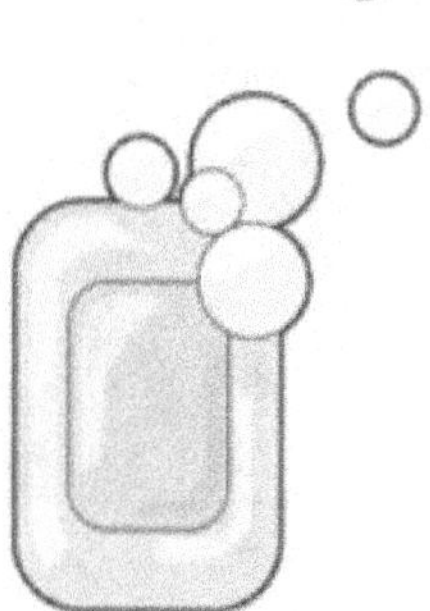

The soap is very bubbly.

pince à linge

כביסה

The clothespin will clip my clothes.

cintre

קוֹלָב

The hanger is hanging my boots.

sèche-cheveux

מייבש שיער

The hairdryer will blow my hair.

shampooing

שַׁמפּוּ

The shampoo is used to clean your hair.

bulle

בּוּעָה

The bubbles are very fun to play in.

brosse

מבְרֶשֶׁת

She is brushing her hair with the brush.

papier toilette

נייר טואלט

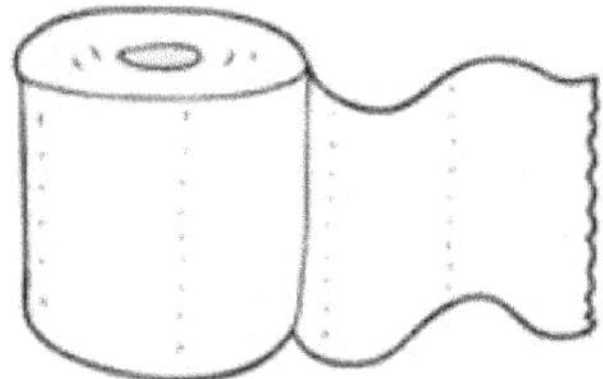

The toilet paper is used to dry your hands.

serviette

מַגֶּבֶת

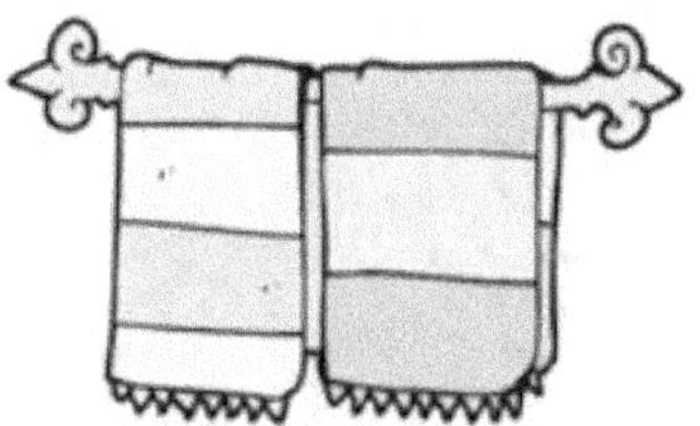

We have two towels on the rack.

corde à linge

קו בגדים

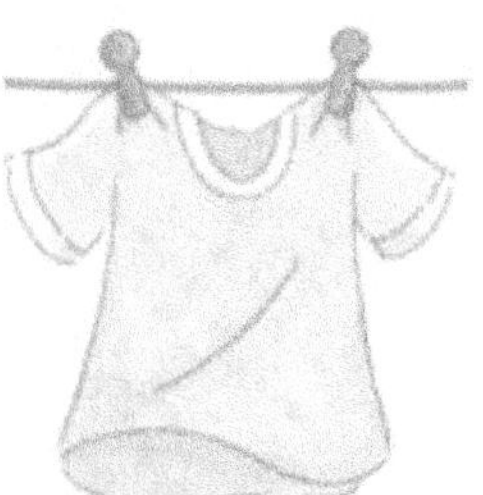

My shirt is hanging on the clothesline.

douche

מִקְלַחַת

The shower is spraying water.

baignoire

אַמבַּטִיָה

The bathtub is comfortable.

lessive

אבקת כביסה

The laundry detergent is used with the washing machine.

seau

דְלִי

Can you help me fill up the bucket?

vadrouilles

מגבים

The mop is used for mopping the floor.

savon liquide

סבון נוזלי

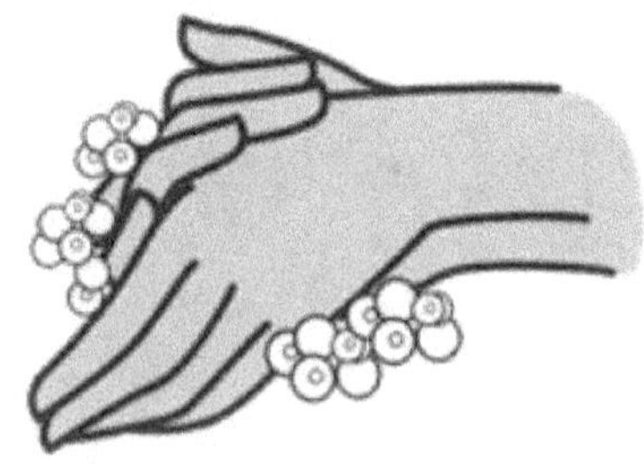

I use soapy water to wash my hands.

lessive en poudre

אבקת כביסה

I will scoop up the washing powder.

sac poubelle

שקית אשפה

The trash bag is full of trash.

poubelle

פח אשפה

You have only to put recylcle trash in the trash can.

You should wash your hands in the sink.

She let her bunny use the toilet.

The washing machine wash your clothes.

She is putting all the clothes into the laundry basket.

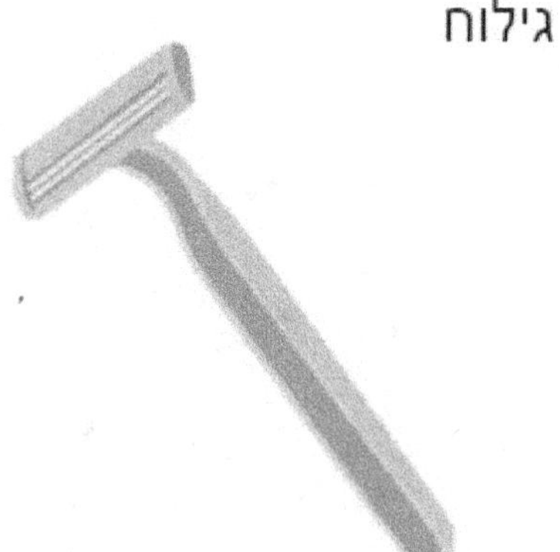

He uses the razor to shave his beard.

The electric razor works faster than the normal one.

crème à raser

קרם גילוח

The shaving cream is fluffy.

bain de bouche

שטיפת פה

The mouthwash smells very lovely.

coton-tige

ניצן כותנה

Q-tip can be used for many things.

brosse à cheveux

מברשת שיער

She brushes her hair with her hairbrush.

peigne

מַסרֵק

Her dad will comb her hair for her.

nettoyant

ניקוי

Put the cap back on the cleanser bottle.

échelle

סוּלָם

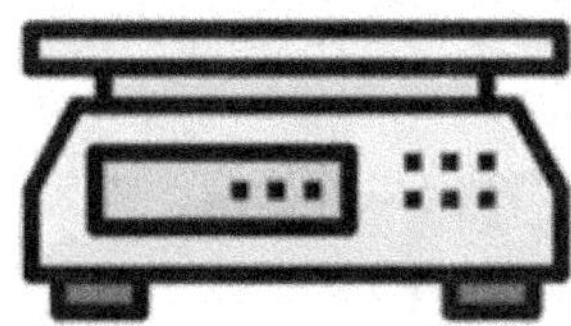

You can measure things on the scale.

papier de soie

נייר טישו

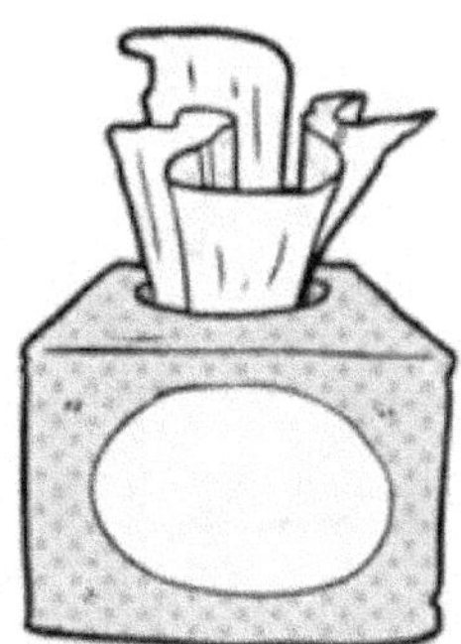

The tissue is on the counter.

jouets de bain

צעצועים לאמבטיה

The little duck is a bath toy.

robinet

בֶּרֶז

The faucet is broken.

miroir

מַרְאָה

He is looking in the mirror.

tapis de bain

שטיח אמבטיה

The bath mat is purple and yellow.